A Heart After God
David

A Devotional

David P. Therrien

DEDICATION

This book is dedicated to those seeking a deeper relationship with God.

CONTENTS

WHY THIS BOOK

The purpose of this book is to bring the reader closer to God. The story of David is a story much like our own story, there are many similarities.

Sometimes reading about other people's experiences can be a help to the one reading.

This is my hope and prayer for you, the reader.

May God bless you as you take this journey and discover things about God, life and yourself that you never knew before.

WEEK ONE

This week you will learn that all of life is a schoolhouse. The events of everyday life, small and large, are used by God to teach life lessons.

MONDAY
DAY 1

Though David is considered a hero of the Bible, he was much like you and me. He grew up a normal boy for his time. He is described as being handsome, of a reddish complexion, beautiful eyes and the youngest of eight sons.

He was born into a time when people were drifting away from God. Samuel was the last of the great judges in Israel and was getting on in years. He passed his office on to his sons who, unfortunately, did not walk with God.

Read I Samuel 8:1-5

The people decided they no longer wanted to be ruled by judges. They wanted a king.

Why did they want to be ruled by a king? (You may find 3 reasons)

1. <u>Samuel was old.</u>

2. _____

3. _____

Summary

The people of Israel no longer respected God's provision for their leadership. They lost faith in Samuel, the judge and rejected his son's authority. But the real problem was that they began to look around at other nations, nations that did not know God. Infatuation with the ways of the world influenced them to think wrongly.

What was their mistake?

_____

_____

Have you ever looked around at the world and desired something God did not provide?

_____

_____

How can you keep from having wandering eyes?

_____

_____

Ask for God's help in prayer.

_____

_____

_____

_____

TUESDAY
DAY 2

We know that Samuel had a problem. Not only was he stressed out from his disobedient sons, but the people had wandered away from God and wanted a king like the other nations. They didn't want to be ruled by judges any longer. Notice how Samuel handled his problem.

Read I Samuel 8:6

Samuel took his problem to the Lord in _____.
Draw an arrow connecting "problem" and "prayer."

Previously, God provided the people with "free" leadership. Now it was going to cost them.

Read vs. 7-17

Notice how they will have to give up so much of what they have in order to support a king.

The people refused to believe that they would regret their decision, even though God told them so. They still wanted to be like other nations.

Read vs. 18-22

The majority of the people were in agreement. It was a nation against a prophet, one man. There is a lot of influence in the majority.

Did you ever find yourself against a majority that went against your Christian convictions?

_____

_____

How did it feel?

_____

How can you prepare yourself for the next time?

_____

_____

Ask for God's help in prayer.

_____

_____

_____

_____

WEDNESDAY
DAY 3

The mistake the people made was to follow their wandering eyes. Mistake number one was to be like other nations. Now they're about to make another mistake.

Read I Samuel 9:1-2

They looked for their first king according to his physical appearance.

What are the two characteristics we see he possessed in v.2?

1. _____

2. _____

Saul was impressive on the outside but had many shortfalls on the inside. He was hot-tempered, given to seasons of depression and was very jealous.

Saul was a man not known for having a strong relationship with God, yet he was the people's choice.

Had the people been walking with God, they would have judged differently. When God looks at a person, He looks at their heart.

Man looks at the outward appearance, but the Lord looks at the heart.
I Samuel 16:7

God is still choosing people to use today. And He is still looking at hearts.

For the eyes of the Lord go throughout the earth to strengthen those whose hearts are fully committed to Him.   I Chronicles 16:9

What can you do to keep your heart right?

_____

_____

Ask for God's help in prayer.

_____

_____

_____

_____

THURSDAY
DAY 4

David was being trained for God's leadership role of the people by doing the work of a shepherd. The shepherd's life was a lonely life. It was a life lived in obscurity and very monotonous. But it was a real life and much needed by the people.

Today we will examine two aspects of his four-fold training ground.

Solitude – The ability to be alone with yourself in order to resolve the inner conflicts in your life. Solitude was one of the teachers God used to prepare David for the throne of Israel.

Have you ever found yourself in solitude and how did you handle it?

_____

_____

Obscurity – This is the place where character is built. Many great men and women of God were first unknown, unseen, unappreciated and unapplauded.

- Gideon
- Moses
- Mary, the mother of Jesus
- The disciples
- David

They all had humble beginnings but went on to greatness because they trusted and obeyed God.

"Those who first accept the silence of obscurity are best qualified to handle the applause of popularity."

Read Psalm 23 meditating on how God is there for you in every one of those situations.

Record a personal thought from each verse.

v.1 _____

v.2 _____

v.3 _____

v.4 _____

v.5 _____

v.6 _____

Ask for God's help in prayer.

_____

_____

_____

_____

FRIDAY
DAY 5

Yesterday we saw that David was being trained for God's leadership role of the people by doing the work of a shepherd. It was a lonely life that included solitude and obscurity.

Today we will examine two more aspects of his four-fold training ground.

Monotony – is being faithful in the menial, insignificant, routine, unexciting and uneventful tasks of daily life.

One man describes this kind of life like flying a plane. It's hours and hours of monotony, punctuated by sheer panic!

Identify some aspects of your life that you would consider monotonous.

_____

_____

Jesus said when you are faithful in a few things, you will be a ruler in many things. Matthew 25:21

Write down how faithfulness in the dull and routine can equip you for greater things in the future.

_____

_____

Reality – is the courage that comes from knowing God is with you.

The Philistines were gathered on an opposite hill from Israel divided by a valley. They were ready for war but no one was making a move. Then, the champion of the Philistines, a nine foot six inch tall giant appeared yelling out threats to Israel. The soldiers shuttered and were afraid to face the giant.

Read I Samuel 17:1-16

Young David showed up to bring lunch to his brothers who were in the army. When he heard the giant's threats he couldn't believe no one would step up and take him. He said he would go up and fight the giant if no one else would. King Saul tried to persuade David that this was no task for a young boy. But David responded;

Read v.34-35

Remember, we said "Reality" was having courage knowing God is with you. Reality is not being afraid of Goliath. If you can take care of the lions and bears in your life, then you won't be afraid when the giants come.

What small things have you handled successfully?

_____

_____

What giants seem to be waiting for you?

_____

_____

Do you see how you've been prepared by the lions and bears for the giants?

Ask for God's help in prayer.

_____

_____

_____

_____

SATURDAY
DAY 6

It is in the little things and in the lonely places that we prove ourselves capable of the big things. This week was a week of introspection on how we handled things in the past and training for how we will handle future things.

If you want to be a person with a large vision, you must cultivate the habit of doing the little things well. They may be detailed reports, daily assignments, homework, chores or anything else that makes up your routine of life.

The test of one's calling is not how they are doing when the spotlight is on them, but when no one is looking Monday through Sunday.

What have you learned about doing the little, monotonous things well?

_____

_____

God is not in a hurry to develop our inner qualities. He knows good things take time. It takes a day to grow a mushroom and sixty years to grow an oak tree.

"The conversion of a soul is the miracle of a moment. The manufacture of a saint is the task of a lifetime." Alan Redpath

Don't be afraid of God's working in your life to prepare you for greater things. It is in the schoolroom of solitude and obscurity that we learn to become men and women of God. It is from the schoolmasters of monotony and reality that we learn to be kings under God's calling. That is how we become like David – men and women after God's own heart.

Read Matthew 25:14-29

What lesson do you see here?

_____

_____

Ask for God's help in prayer to apply this week's lessons.

_____

_____

_____

_____

WEEK TWO

This week we are going to see that God has a plan. He is never taken by surprise and always knows what His next move is going to be. Even our mistakes cannot thwart what God wants to do.

MONDAY
DAY 7

King Saul was a man who proved that if you get away from a personal relationship with God, your whole temperament can change for the worse. This negative change can result in the disqualification of a position of leadership.

Saul's three major mistakes
1. He made a terrible decision. He offered a burnt offering to God without waiting for Samuel the religious leader of Israel.

Read I Samuel 13:8-13

You could say Saul was impatient. Only the religious leader could offer sacrifices to God but Saul couldn't wait.
This shows us that whatever we do for God, it must be done His way.

2. He pronounced a death sentence upon his son, Jonathan.
Saul took a count of his army and was told Jonathan and his shield bearer were not in the camp. He then passed this statute.

Read I Samuel 14:24-28

Saul continues to behave outside of his role as king.

3. He openly disobeyed God by keeping some of the spoils of war. God told him to go to war with the Amalekites and take no prisoners or spoils.

Read I Samuel 15:1-9

Saul thought, why waste all of this good livestock. God's plan is flawed but my plan makes more sense.

Saul made some serious mistakes.

Look back at no. 1. Did you ever find yourself impatient with God and taken matters into your own hands?

Look back at no. 2. Did you ever say something that would affect another person in a negative way?

Look back at no. 3. Did you ever think in any given situation that your plan was better than God's plan?

What lesson do you see here?

_____

_____

Ask for God's help in prayer in any of these three areas.

_____

_____

_____

_____

TUESDAY
DAY 8

There is a true to life principle that I think we can all attest to. And that is, man panic and God provides. Have you ever found that to be true in your own life?

We have to remember, God always has a _____.

Even before there was sin in the world, God had a plan for salvation. Jesus was the
Lamb that was slain from the creation of the world. Revelation 13:3

Saul's mistakes had disqualified him from his position but God knew what He was going to do. He already had a man in mind, young David.

A good lesson to remember is;
When a man or woman of God fails, nothing of God fails.
When our lives are altered by the unexpected, nothing of God is altered.

Samuel had not yet realized that God had rejected Saul from being king. God gave Samuel a task which caused him to fear for his life.
Read I Samuel 16:1-2

There will be times in our own lives that will cause us to fear. What should one do in this case?

Look to the Lord and His strength; seek His face always. Psalm 105.4

When Peter got out of the boat in Matthew 14 and walked on the water, he began to sink because he took his eyes off Jesus and looked at the water.

God didn't seem interested in Samuel's fears. He just told him what to do and Samuel did it.
Read vs. 3-4

Doing God's will doesn't require agreement, just obedience. This is how we live in faith toward Him. Unfortunately, in our modern church today, people find it very easy to disagree with God and therefore, disobey Him. For convenience sake, people gossip, steal and live together as married when they are not married. This is living way outside of faith and therefore, can never be pleasing to God.

What lesson do you see here for you?

_____

_____

Ask for God's help in prayer in any of this.

_____

_____

_____

_____

WEDNESDAY
DAY 9

The Bible is filled with many promises from God. Did you ever wonder why He gives us so many promises? He gives them to help us through life's situations. The more you know them and believe them, the more they will help you.

A very beautiful promise was spoken through the prophet, Jeremiah.

I know the plans I have for you declares the Lord, plans to prosper you and not to harm you, plans to give you a hope and a future. Jeremiah 29:11

We saw yesterday that God told Samuel to go to the house of Jesse for there he would find the next king of Israel. Though somewhat fearful for his life because of King Saul finding out, he went in obedience.

Read I Samuel 16:4-13

According to v.7, on what basis does God choose a person for His service?

_____

_____

Samuel is learning a valuable lesson, which was also proven by Saul. The outward appearance of a person does not necessarily reveal what kind of a person her or she is on the inside.

"To see beyond someone's age or their size or the level of intelligence; to see worth and value down deep inside; that's the kind of vision that Samuel with God's help finally demonstrates at this point." *Chuck Swindoll*

Write down the name of anyone in your life you need to look at differently?

_____

_____

What changes must you make in order to do so?

_____

_____

Ask for God's help in prayer.

_____

_____

_____

_____

THURSDAY
DAY 10

After David was anointed king by Samuel, he didn't go downtown and try on crowns. He went back to the pastures to shepherd sheep. There were also times when Saul, who was still acting as king and hadn't been removed yet by God, sent for David to play his harp and soothe his troubled spirit.
Read I Samuel 16:14-23

David had great humility. One day he would be tending sheep in the field and another day he would be playing music in the king's court. His life seemed to be one of promotion, demotion and promotion again. But he never complained.
Sometimes as people, when we are raised up, we never want to be lowered again.

Have you ever arrived at a higher position in life and then refused to do the menial things you once did before? What was it?

_____

_____

How did you feel when asked to do the menial thing?

_____

_____

What was David's secret to having this ability? He obviously knew the Scriptures and applied them to his life.

Those who wait for the Lord will gain new strength, they will mount up with wings like eagles. They will run and not get tired. They will walk and not become weary. Isaiah 40:31

In what area of your life can you apply this principle?

_____

_____

Ask for God's help in prayer.

_____

_____

_____

_____

FRIDAY
DAY 11

Young David was truly a Godly boy who would grow up to be a Godly man. He not only knew the Scriptures but he applies them to his life. He made them his authority and this enabled him to be groomed by God to be the next king of Israel. Not only was he going to be the next king but he would be the greatest king.

Fill in the beginning of this verse from yesterday.

"_____

will gain new strength."

Today and tomorrow we will look at three lessons that we can learn from his life.

The first lesson is:
    1. Be open to God.
When we wait on the Lord we are open to God's solutions which may seem strange but always right.
This means I will;
- Go where God tells me
- Do what God commands me
- Trust Him at all times.

Is there something in your life right now where one or more of these may apply? What is it?

_____

_____

We must remember that God's Word is always there to direct our path.

The second lesson is:

2.   Be ready for God's promotions which may be sudden and and surprising. That's why you should never quit on God. He will come through when you least expect it. When you and I have exhausted all our resources, God is ready to reveal His.

Paul acknowledged God's wisdom over man's:
The foolishness of God is wiser than men, and the weakness of God is stronger than men. I Corinthians 1:25
Therefore:
I will rather boast about my weaknesses, that the power of Christ may dwell in me. I Corinthians 12:9

Is there an area of your life right now where you need Scripture to direct you?

_____

_____

What is the Scripture?

_____

_____

Ask for God's help in prayer.

_____

_____

_____

_____

SATURDAY
DAY 12

Yesterday we looked at two of the three lessons we learned from the life of David this week. From yesterday lesson no. 1 was;

    1. Be _____.

Lesson no. 2 was;

    2. Be ready _____

Which may be sudden and surprising.

We will end this week with the third lesson.

    3. Be sensitive to God selecting you for a task.

Samuel looked at each of Jesse's sons but it wasn't until he saw the last one and the least suspected that he recognized God's choice for the next king of Israel.

God has a timetable for what He is doing as well as a plan.

When you are sensitive to God's call on your life, you forget about the surrounding circumstances.

Illustration:

1809 was a very good year but those who were alive then didn't know it. Napoleon was making his march across Austria and conquering everything in his path. People feared the whole world would fall into his hands.

During that time babies were born. William Gladstone, Alfred Tennyson, Oliver Wendell Holmes, Edgar Allen Po and Abraham Lincoln. The lives of these statesmen and writers and thinkers would mark the beginning of an era. But nobody cared about those nobodies while Napoleon was on the march.

The strange thing is that today, only history buffs could name one battle Napoleon fought in Austria. But there is not a life of a person alive today that has not been touched in some way by the lives of theose other men.

It is easy to focus on the "Sauls" of life and forget that God always has a plan. And that plan was formulated before the creation of the world. And we are part of that plan. And in spite of how bad the world may seem, God's plan will be victorious.

Read II Timothy 1:8-9

What kind of a calling did God call you with?

_____

What does this mean to you?

_____

_____

Ask God for help in prayer.

_____

_____

_____

_____

WEEK THREE

This week we are going to learn about music. Music is a gift from God for the soothing of the soul. Perhaps you have noticed that you enjoy different types of music depending on the mood you are in or the circumstances around you.
We will see David's gift of music and how God used it.

MONDAY
DAY 13

I sometimes say that music is magic. I don't mean magic in the sense of the occult but in the sense that it has the power to affect the feelings. Music eases the soul.

Music on the earth began in Genesis 4. Verse 21 tells us that
Jubal was the father of all those who play the pipe.

God loves music. Right in the middle of our Bible we have 150 songs called psalms. More than half of them were written by David. It is as if God were saying, "Sing them and sing them often and learn them well. They are My songs."

Though David was anointed king of Israel, God had not yet removed Saul from the throne. But he began to take a turn for the worst personally and spiritually.
Read I Samuel 16:14-15

When the Spirit of the Lord departed from people in the Old Testament, it left them in a weakened state.
Samson did not know that the Lord had departed from him. Judges 16:20
At this point, Samson had lost his great physical strength.

David prayer to God;
Do not take Thy Holy Spirit from me. Psalm 51:11

The good news is that God does not take away His Spirit from believers today. We are now indwelt and sealed with the Holy Spirit of Promise. Ephesians 1:13.

Though the Holy Spirit is no longer taken from believers, when the believer sins the Spirit is grieved.

Is there a weakness in your life that, when you give in to it, it grieves the Spirit?

_____

_____

Ask God for help in prayer.

_____

_____

_____

_____

TUESDAY
DAY 14

Saul had a problem. There were two very important things in his life he did not take seriously.
1. His role as king
2. God as his authority

God said to the people through the prophet Zechariah;
I am exceedingly jealous. Zechariah 8:2

This is a measure of how great God's love is for us. He wants no one else nor does He wish we would want anyone else.
Read I Samuel 16:15

The Holy Spirit not only left Saul but God allowed an evil spirit to terrorize him. The result was that he fell into a depression with fits of insanity. His imagination drove him to madness.

There is never a good result that can be found when one walks away from their relationship with God.

Did you ever find yourself in a situation where your imagination was running wild? Did you begin to imagine things that were not true? Could you be slipping away from God in your personal relationship with Him?

How different from the man Isaiah spoke about;
You (God) will keep in perfect peace him whose mind is steadfast because he tusts in You. Isaiah 26:3

What can you do to keep your mind in perfect peace?

_____

_____

Try to avoid the mistakes that Saul made.
1. Know your God appointed role in life and take it seriously.
2. Always see God as your final authority.

Be on the lookout for some of those ill feelings that terrorized Saul. If you recognize any of them beginning to come into your life, get back with God as quickly as you can.

Ask God for help in prayer.

_____

_____

_____

_____

WEDNESDAY
DAY 15

The difference that we have seen between Saul and David is that David always put his trust in the Lord and Saul lost his trust and began to believe only in himself. Yet, the Bible is very clear on the benefits of trusting God for life's situations.

You who fear the Lord trust in the Lord. He is their help and their shield.
Psalm 115:11

What do you think is the benefit here?

_____

_____

He who trusts in the Lord, lovingkindness shall surround him. Psalm 32:10

What do you think is the benefit here?

_____

_____

He who gives attention to the word shall find good and blessed is he who trust in the Lord. Proverbs 16:20

What do you think is the benefit here?

_____

_____

Because of Saul's lack of trust, his malady grew severe and even those around him realized he needed help.
Read vs. 16-17

Write down the kind of music you like to listen to according to the mood you are in.

_____

_____

As humans, we can run the full gamut of emotions. But it is not only music that we need to calm our spirit. We also need to pray.

Ask God for help in prayer.

_____

_____

_____

_____

THURSDAY
DAY 16

Music has always played a part in the heritage of people all over the world. It was used in a triumphal march after battle, feasts and festivals, time of grieving and time of gladness, marriages and even the shepherd played his flute while watching the sheep.

We will see that good character travels.
Read I Samuel 16:18

Notice David's credentials:
- Skillful musician
- Brave man
- A warrior
- Speaks well
- Fine looking
- The Lord is with him

It is true that a person's bad reputation can precede him, but thankfully so can a good reputation.

What are some of the good qualities you are known for?
(Don't be shy, this is an honest evaluation of yourself)

_____

_____

When God finds a person with a good character, He promotes that person.
Do you see a man skilled in his work? He will stand before kings. He will not stand before obscure men. Proverbs 22:29

This tells me that whatever it is that I do, I should strive to be my best at it.

What is something or things you are good at?

_____

_____

Do your best to get better and then pray for God's help.

Ask God for help in prayer to be better at what you do.

_____

_____

_____

_____

FRIDAY
DAY 17

Never discount anything you have learned or accomplished in your past. There are things you have learned in the world even before you were saved that God will allow you to bring into the service of His kingdom.

It could be in the realm of music, carpentry, business, administration, art and drama, domestic abilities, finances, etc.

Nothing you have learned in your past is insignificant in the kingdom of God.

Remember when Saul was plagued with an evil spirit and was told that young David was a skillful musician? Because of his skill, he received a promotion.

Read I Samuel 16:19-23

David was promoted to court musician and Saul's personal armor bearer. But there were times that Saul sent David back to the sheep after David played and refreshed him.

David never complained about the tasks, whether in the field or in the court, that he was given to do.

What service could you provide to the kingdom of God that you were good at in the world?

_____

_____

I once had a man come to me who wanted to be a pastor. I said okay and gave him a menial task to do. He eventually quit. That man will never know what it means to be a servant-leader. God doesn't need celebrities. The first step is humility.

If you desire a role in leadership, that is a good thing. But remember, a good leader begins by being a good servant.

Ask God for help in prayer to be better at what you do.

_____

_____

_____

_____

SATURDAY
DAY 18

In eternity past the angels worshipped God with singing at the creation of the universe.
Read Job 38

What were the sons of God (angels) doing in v.7?

_____

_____

John's vision of heaven:
And I saw something like a sea of glass mixed with fire, and those who had been victorious over the beast and his image and the number of his name, standing on the sea of glass, holding harps of God.
And they sang the song of Moses, the bond-servant of God, and the song of the Lamb, saying, "Great and marvelous are Your works, O Lord God, the Almighty; Righteous and true are Your ways, King of the nations!
Revelation 15:2-3

Genuine worship is the blending of the Word of God and the music of God. Music is not only given to soothe the soul but to give worship to God. The longest book in the Bible, Psalm 119, is a song.

The songs we sing are to make us conscious of God. It raises our level of awareness of His presence and prepares us to receive His Word.

God provided soft music for a hard heart through David. Christ is our Shepherd and we are His sheep needing the music of His voice. That is why we cannot underestimate the power and effect of our worship that is sung for our benefit and for His praise.

List one or two of your favorite worship songs.

_____

_____

Why is it your favorite? What does it do for you?

_____

_____

Ask God for help in prayer to be better at your worship.

_____

_____

_____

_____

WEEK FOUR

This week we are going to talk about giants. Do giants exist? Sure they do. They are those big, scary, threatening figures that loom up ahead. Sometimes they get too close for comfort. But there is a way to handle them and not only handle them, but defeat them.

MONDAY
DAY 19

Before going into a battle in life against a giant, there are two things to remember.
1. No matter how big the giant is, God is greater.
2. No matter how powerful the giant is, God is all-powerful.
The scene:
The battleground between the armies of Israel and the Philistines was like a canyon. A stream ran nearby where David retrieved five smooth stones to take into his battle with Goliath.
Read I Samuel 17:1-4

The principle still rings true. Man looks at the outward appearance but God looks at the heart. Outwardly, a nine foot six inch giant could be very intimidating.
Read vs. 5-7

Goliath certainly looked intimidating.
What do you think your feelings would be at this scene?

_____

_____

Giants **always** look intimidating. That's why they're called "giants."
Goliath not only looked intimidating but he also looked perfectly protected. He looked indestructible. He also had a weapon that was matchless.
What was his weapon according to v.7?

_____

How do you think the soldiers felt when they saw this giant?

_____

Think of a giant you have faced in your own life. Was it intimidating or terrifying? Is there a giant facing you right now?

A good Scripture to take into any battle is;
> *No weapon formed against you will prosper...* Isaiah 54:17

Ask God for help in prayer to face your giant.

_____

_____

_____

_____

TUESDAY
DAY 20

The giant in David's life was very much like the giants in your life. He looked intimidating, indestructible and like the obvious victor. Giants always give the impression that they are going to win and they have the tools to back it up. But remember, giants are natural problems and the Christian has spiritual resources.

Read I Samuel 17:8-9

Like any giant in life, Goliath challenges the faith of the believers. The positive thing about giants is that they cause us to be introspective and evaluate the depth of our faith in God.

Paul said to the Corinthians;
> *Test yourselves to see if you are in the faith; examine yourselves!*
> II Corinthians 13:5

Read vs. 10-11

Notice the power of words. Were you ever frightened by the words someone said to you?
How did it make you feel?

_____

_____

Read vs. 16

Goliath's challenge was relentless.
Some giants are like that, they just won't quit. Their intention is to cause you fear, worry, lust, selfishness, greed, gossip, etc.
These impulses hammer the believer every single day.

What have you been hammered with lately?

_____

_____

Ask God for help in prayer to face your giant.

_____

_____

_____

_____

WEDNESDAY
DAY 21

The giant has a scheme. His greatest weapon is not his appearance nor his strength. His greatest weapon is his strategy. And that strategy is to get you to compare your strength to his strength. It is a mind game.

So far, the only involvement David had in the battle was what he heard in reports from the front line. Jesse sent young David to the battle with some food for his brothers and to see how they were doing.

Read I Samuel 17:17-18

David entered the battle as an errand boy. He had no intention to get into the fight.
Some of God's greatest servant's never intended to be involved in the work of God. God has a way of scooping people out of the world and putting them into his service.
The Apostle Paul, the Disciples, Gideon, Moses and many others were chosen by God to this way.

Read vs. 20-24

David hears the challenge. The soldiers also hear the challenge and flee. The real giant here is the opportunity to serve and glorify God. The soldiers ran from this opportunity. They thought this particular opportunity was just bigger than them.

Did you ever think, the bigger the threat, the bigger the opportunity?
Did you ever face an intimidating giant and fail to see it as an opportunity? What was it?

_____

_____

Ask God for help in prayer to see the opportunity instead of the giant.

_____

_____

_____

_____

THURSDAY
DAY 22

The problem with the men of Israel was not that they were poorly trained or ill-equipped. They were actually a powerful fighting force. The problem was how they saw the battle. They kept staring at the giant.

Read I Samuel 17:25

The lesson learned here today is what you keep looking at could destroy you. (read that again).

The Apostle John commented on this fact.

For all that is in the world, the lust of the flesh and the lust of the eyes and the boastful pride of life is not from the Father, but it is from the world. And the world is passing away, and also its lusts; but the one who does the will of God abides forever. I John 2:16

These are three dangerous occupations:
1. Feeling – the lust of the flesh
2. Seeing – the lust of the eyes
3. Wanting – the pride of life

Which one of these have you been recently battling with?

_____

Ask God for help in prayer in this area.

_____

_____

_____

_____

FRIDAY
DAY 23

Giants can never be ignored or left alone. That's because they have an imposing presence and are threatening. No one should have to live in those conditions.

We saw yesterday that the giant is now coming up and shouting his threats and the soldiers were spell-bound.

Read I Samuel 17:26-30

If you tolerate a giant in your life, he will take over your territory. The real battle is no on the battlefield but in the mind.

What are the brothers doing to David in v. 28?

_____

_____

Have your ever been discouraged by others for wanting to do a good thing? Those who discourage are usually those who do not want to get involved anyway. Sometimes they don't stop at discouragement but lead to criticism also.

But David didn't enter that battle. He knew who the real enemy was.

Sometimes the Church today and many Christians are fighting the wrong battle. The Church should be fighting the kingdom of darkness but often finds itself fighting other Christians.

Jesus said we are here to save people, not fight them. Our fight is a spiritual warfare.

The Apostle Paul said;

For our struggle is not against flesh and blood, but against the rulers, against the powers, against the world forces of this darkness, against the spiritual forces of wickedness in the heavenly places. Ephesians 6:12

What will you do when you come up against discouragement from now on?

_____

_____

Ask God for help in prayer when you face discouragement.

_____

_____

_____

_____

SATURDAY
DAY 24

Like a powerful river has a source, so does ones strength. Though a young boy, David had strength, more strength of mind than of body. David had a good strategy when facing huge opposition.
1. He didn't compare his strength to the giant's.
2. He remembered the smaller victories from the past.

Read I Samuel 17:33-37

Your smaller victories are stepping stones to your larger victories.
What are some of your smaller victories?

_____

_____

Learn from your failures but celebrate your victories.

In v.37, where does David say his victory came from?

_____

Read vs. 42-44

The giant's weapon – intimidation.
What has intimidation stopped you from doing in the past?

_____

_____

Read v. 45

What was David's weapon?

_____

Read vs. 48-51

God showed David the giant's vulnerability. By keeping his eyes o God and not the giant, he was able to hear from God and know what to do.

No victory is insignificant. Our memories of past victories give us the confidence to face our present battles. When God does something small or great in your life, do not forget it!

Ask God for help in prayer to remember past victories.

WEEK FIVE

Friendship is not something we ever want to take lightly. And having an intimate friend is a rare find. An intimate friend is one who you can trust at all costs. They are with you through thick and thin, highs and lows. This is where we will find David this week. He has found an intimate friend to help him through his difficult times.

MONDAY
DAY 25

After David killed Goliath he went through a very hard time. You would think that being a hero would be a wonderful experience. Well it is, except when your boss is a very jealous man.

David experienced two types of responses for his heroic feat.

1. He received praise from the people.
2. He received suspicion from Saul.

Saul's imagination had run wild and his jealousy caused him to make continual threats on David's life. David had encountered another giant.

Read I Samuel 17:52-58

David slew the giant and was introduced to king Saul.

At this time David is unsuspecting of the kind of man Saul was and what he would turn out to be.

What the Bible says about jealousy:

For jealousy enrages a man, and he will not spare in the day of vengeance.
Proverbs 6:34

Wrath is fierce and anger is a flood, but who can stand before jealousy?
Proverbs 27:4

But God provided something that David needed, and it wasn't an escape or a way out. It was an intimate friend.

How have you been that intimate friend to someone in need?

_____

_____

There are four aspects to being an intimate friend that we will note this week. Remember, it is important to have such a friend and equally important to be that friend.

Ask God for help in prayer to be an intimate friend to someone. If you need one, ask for Him to provide one.

_____

_____

_____

_____

TUESDAY
DAY 26

An intimate friend is more than a friend. An intimate friend is a willing sacrifice.
Read I Samuel 18:1-4

In v.4 what did Jonathan do to demonstrate his love for David?

_____

_____

In those days armor was owned by a fortunate few. Perhaps today it would be like giving up your car.
Intimate friends are never stingy with their possessions.

Have you ever given or received something as a token of true friendship?

_____

_____

You can never impose on an intimate friend. An intimate friend is there to assist whenever and in whatever is needed. In intimate friendship unselfishness prevails.

Ask God for help in prayer to recognize intimate friendship.

_____

_____

_____

_____

WEDNESDAY
DAY 27

An intimate friend is not a fair-weather friend. An intimate friend won't talk against you when you are not around.
An intimate friend is a defense before others.

Read I Samuel 19:1-9

Why do you think Saul's attitude changed toward David? v.9

_____

_____

Saul still saw David as his enemy though David was out fighting battles for him Saul's real enemy was jealousy.

The friendship of Jonathan:
- He stood up for what was right.
- He did not let sentimentality overrule righteousness.

This is not so common today. In many cases, sentimentality overrules righteousness.

Perhaps you have been torn between standing up for what is right and being sentimental to a friend. Be a friend and stand up for truth.

Faithful are the wounds of a friend,
But deceitful are the kisses of an enemy. Proverbs 27:6

Remember, being the king's son, he is heir to the throne. Yet, in Jonathan we find that he is not jealous and does not desire anything but what is right.

Where something is right, there is also something that is wrong. This is where conflict comes in. We often forget the Christian life is filled with conflict.

It is a fight – *Fight the good fight of faith.* I Timothy 6:12

It is a warfare – *For the weapons of our warfare are not of the flesh, but divinely powerful for the destructions of fortresses.* I Corinthians 2:10

It is a battle – *The battle is the Lord's.* I Samuel 7:14

It is a boxing match – *I box in such a way as not beating the air.*
I Corinthians 9:26

Therefore, an intimate friend is not afraid of the battle.

Who is there who needs you to stand with them in some way?

_____

Ask God for help in prayer to help you to stand strong for someone.

_____

_____

_____

_____

THURSDAY
DAY 28

Intimate friends give each other complete freedom. This is the freedom to be yourself, especially in times of grief. An intimate friend identifies with the feelings of their friend and does not deny them.
Read I Samuel 20

In v.41, how are David and Jonathan expressing their grief?

_____

_____

When your heart is broken, you can bleed all over an intimate friend and your friend will understand.
You won't get a Bible lesson on how to control your emotions or how to have more faith. You are free to be express yourself.

In v.42, who is in the middle of David and Jonathan's friendship?

_____

Ask God for help in prayer that He would be in the middle of your intimate friendship.

_____

_____

_____

_____

FRIDAY
DAY 29

An intimate friend is a constant source of encouragement. Because it is so easy to be occupied with the giants, an intimate friend gets your eyes back on the Lord.
Read I Samuel 23:1-18

In v.16, what did Jonathan do for David?

_____

_____

To encourage him in the Lord means to bring God into the picture. He gave David a new perspective. An intimate friend not only gives good advice but an intimate friend gives God.

You owe it to your intimate friend to grow in the grace and knowledge of Jesus Christ and Scripture so you can provide the promises of God need for any given situation.
It is better to give a divine viewpoint than be sentimental.

Make a commitment today to grow in the Scriptures so you can be a blessing to others.

Ask God for help in prayer to grow in divine wisdom to help others to face their giants.

_____

_____

_____

_____

SATURDAY
DAY 30

We learned quite a bit about what is an intimate friendship. We have been challenged to act righteously over sentimentality. We learned that the Christian life is filled with conflicts. We must be the kind of people who stand for truth.

We are not talking about a collection of friends. We are talking about a special, intimate friend.

A man of too many friends comes to ruin, but there is a friend who sticks closer than a brother. Proverbs 18:24

This is the friendship we see between David and Jonathan.

Oil and perfume make the heart glad, so a man's counsel is sweet to his friend.
                                                            Proverbs 27:9

Good, Godly advice is refreshing to a friend in need.

Summary:
1. An intimate friend is a willing sacrifice.
2. An intimate friend is a loyal defense before others.
3. Intimate friends give each other complete freedom to be themselves.
4. An intimate friend is a constant source of encouragement and never leaves God out of the picture.

Intimate friendship is not a matter of quantity of time spent together but of quality of time spent together.

If you don't have one – get one.

If you are not one – be one.

Ask for God's help in prayer for an intimate friendship.

_____

_____

_____

WEEK FIVE

This week we are going to learn about crutches. Crutches are things we lean on to hold us up. The danger of this is that crutches can be removed. When that happens, what is left to learn on?

MONDAY
DAY 31

It is very easy to go through life and without even realizing it, build your confidence and security on what would be considered matchsticks. We know them as crutches.

A crutch is simply something to lean on. We are going to see that David had some crutches and God removed them.

David was in the service of King Saul. He was mighty in battle and a skilled musician. With these two talents he served Saul well. But Saul became jealous of David to the point where he sought to kill him.

Imagine the pressure of going to work knowing that the person you work for is trying to kill you! Now that's pressure.

The life of David teaches us that living in humility, integrity and dependability do not always pay off in a comfortable way, though it is still the right thing to do.

Read I Samuel 19:9-10

Notice the difference in the two men.

Saul had an instrument of destruction in his hand.

What was it?

_____

David had an instrument of healing in his hand.

What was it?

_____

Our instrument of choice says a lot about an individual. There are so many to choose from. Gossip or prayer, helping or hurting, giving or taking, etc.

The first crutch taken from David was a good position.

Read vs. 11-12

How did David escape for his life?

_____

_____

When David served in Saul's army, he was a soldier, a hero and faithful. Now, he will never again serve in Saul's army.

Have you ever had a position removed from you?

_____

_____

Ask for God's help in prayer to hold you up.

_____

_____

_____

_____

TUESDAY
DAY 32

David had received the daughter of King Saul in marriage as a gift for killing Goliath. Marriage is an intimate relationship and the dissolution of a marriage is a painful thing.

The second crutch taken from David was his wife, Michal.
Read I Samuel 19:14-18

David's wife lied for him but it didn't help the situation. But then she lied about him in v.17.
What did she say?

_____

_____

David will never lie with his wife again. She had basically walked away from him. David has now lost two important parts of his life, his job and his wife.

David didn't throw a pity party for himself. He did what a man after God's heart would do.
Read v.18

What did David do?

_____

_____

Naioth was a place of many dwellings and the prophets lived there. Therefore, that was a good place to hide.
When being pursued by life's circumstances we often seek a place of refuge. We must be careful in what we choose or where we go. There are places that look safe but they are not. They are places that actually lead to sin.

Where do you go to find refuge in times of crisis?

_____

_____

Ask for God's help in prayer to lead you to the proper place of refuge in your trials, the place where God is.

_____

_____

_____

_____

WEDNESDAY
DAY 33

God is removing David's crutches one by one. First his position, then his wife. Now God is going to remove his spiritual counselor.
Read I Samuel 20:1

Who was David's spiritual counselor?

_____

David is now back with his intimate friend, Jonathan. He was losing everything he had a habit of leaning on.

It is only human to build one's life on that which can hold you up in a physical, social or emotional sense.
A job could be a physical crutch.
A mate could be a social crutch.
A counselor could be an emotional crutch.

God's Word tells us that there are wrong things to lean on.
> _He who trusts in riches will fall._ Proverbs 11:28
> _He who trusts in his own heart is a fool._ Proverbs 28:26
> _Cursed is the man who trusts in mankind and makes flesh his strength._
> Jeremiah 17:5

As wrong as it is to lean on these things, we do it so easily. We must be careful we do not depend only on them.

What crutches have you leaned on in the past?

_____

_____

Are they still around today and are they still your crutches? Sometimes these things do work for a while but they will not always be there. That is why we need the Lord to lean on. He will never leave you nor forsake you.

Ask for God's help in prayer to lean on Jesus in time of need.

_____

_____

_____

_____

THURSDAY
DAY 34

So far David lost his job, wife and spiritual counselor. That's a lot!
You would think, that's enough. But God is not through yet.
His fourth crutch to be removed is his friend.
Read I Samuel 20:1-3

David feels he is one step away from death.
It is an awful feeling to see no future for your life. You can only see today but tomorrow looks bleak, hopeless, like death.
Read v.42

For safety's sake, David and Jonathan had to part company. David was going to be on his own now. No job, no wife, no spiritual counselor and now no friend.
This is an awful place to be yet, many people, at one time or another feel that they've been in the same place as David.
Remember,
If God is removing the crutches, it is not the end of the road. God is making a way and preparing you for greater blessings. He has a brighter future in the making and you are being prepared for it.

Ask for God's help in prayer if your crutches are being removed.

_____

_____

_____

_____

FRIDAY
DAY 35

This last crutch that is going to be removed from David comes as a real surprise. This is one that would seem so important, not even considered a crutch. But God's thoughts are not our thoughts and His ways are higher than our ways.

For as the heavens are higher than the earth, so are My ways higher than your ways and My thoughts than your thoughts. Isaiah 55:9

The fifth crutch that is going to be removed from David is his self-reputation.
Read I Samuel 21:10-15

Gath was the place where Goliath was from. David had previously killed that giant. He was deliberately walking into the headquarters of the Philistines.
In v.13, how did David lose his reputation?

_____

_____

When our crutches are removed, we begin to act differently. When you go through life leaning on things and those things are taken from you, you can begin to act crazy. (do dumb things)

An old country and western song says;
"When everything's gone, anything goes."

Ask for God's help in prayer when you don't know what to do.

_____

_____

_____

_____

SATURDAY
DAY 36

As you can see, crutches are a serious matter. They are not the perfect solution for life's dilemmas because they can be removed and then what do you have – nothing.

Three warnings for those who lean on crutches.
    1.   Crutches become substitutes for God.
The eternal God is a dwelling place, and underneath are the everlasting arms.
Deuteronomy 33:27

    2.   Crutches keep us in a human perspective.
Set your mind on the things above, not on the things that are on earth.
Colossians 3:2

    3.   Crutches provide only a temporary help.
        I will never leave you or forsake you. (Jesus)   Hebrews 13:5

"Things were always meant to be used by man, to be external to him. They were given to serve him. The heart of man was made to be filled by God."   A. W. Tozer

Is there a crutch being removed from your life right now?

_____

You have a choice. You can look around for another crutch, someone or something to lean on – or you can lean on God and God alone.
The Psalmist said;
 But as for me, I trust in Thee, O Lord, I say, thou art my God. Psalm 31:14

Ask for God's help in prayer to be your crutch.

_____

_____

_____

WEEK SEVEN

Did you ever have the feeling that life had bottomed out? You know,
you have sunk just about as low as you can sink.
David's crutches had been removed, we found him playing the
madman. He had lost his reputation. Let's see what happens next.

MONDAY
DAY 37

David left Gath and King Achish and was on the run again.
Read I Samuel 22:1-2

What kind of people gathered themselves to David?

_____

_____

What do you think it is like living in a cave?

_____

_____

Living in a cave would appear to the natural mind the end of the road. No light, no food, no plans, no help. It is a cold and dark place to be. David had lost everything that was important to him.
The good news is that he hadn't lost God.

David wrote Palm 142 demonstrating that he is a man with a heart after God.

> _I cry aloud with my voice to the Lord;_
> _I make supplication with my voice to the Lord._

David was learning, when the sovereign God brings us to nothing, it is to revive our lives, not to end them. _Circle "revive"_

The fiery darts of the devil say, " This is the end."
God says, "This is a new direction."

God is still working in David's life. He brought back in his father who overlooked him in the pasture or his brothers who ridiculed him at the battlefield, and He brought him some new friends.

Be available to what God may be doing in your life when He leads you to a place that looks like it has no future. The cave is the training ground for greater things.

Can you think of a cave experience that God has led you to in the past?

_____

_____

Ask for God's help in prayer to be your crutch.

_____

_____

_____

_____

TUESDAY
DAY 38

Sometimes God works in our lives in ways we least expect. We want patience so He puts us in a line. We need rest so He lets us get sick. He works in ways we least expect. This is what He is going to do with David. God brought all kinds of malcontents into his life.
Read I Samuel 22:1-2

These people had issues! Why would God bring people like this into David's life after all he had been through? Perhaps because it gave David something noble to do. He would be their commander and would train them into a mighty fighting force.

The best way to get through your own problems is to help someone else with theirs.

How much is this like Jesus when He cried out:
Come to me all who are weary and heavy laden, and I will give you rest.
Matthew 11:28

Who were some people that God brought into your life to minister to?

_____

_____

When that happened, how did you feel after you ministered to them?

_____

_____

Solomon wrote a beautiful psalm depicting the character of the Lord.

For He will deliver the needy when he cries for help, the afflicted also and him who has no helper.

He will have compassion on the poor and needy, and the lives of the needy He will save.

He will rescue their life from oppression and violence, and their blood will be precious in His sight. Psalm 72:12-14

Ask for God's help in prayer to be sensitive to the needs of others in spite of your own difficulties.

_____

_____

_____

_____

WEDNESDAY
DAY 39

Saul was a terrible king. He overtaxed and mistreated the people. These were people who were hurting, couldn't pay their bills and became bitter about life. These were the people in David's cave.
Read I Samuel 22:1-2 again

So David ended up with a cave full of malcontents. It is bad enough feeling like a worm. Now he has four hundred more worms who crawled in there to be with him.

Here is the key to any cave situation: "God is always working."
Write that key down here.

_____

That is a truth you never want to let go of, and this is why.
The cave went from a place of hiding to a place of training.
These malcontents will become David's mighty men of valor!

At this point, it is not so much what David did, but what he didn't do. He didn't walk away. It is so easy to just "walk away" when things don't look good.

"Winners don't walk away, winners stay at the task."
Write that truth down here.

_____

_____

People become winners when they continue to learn, train and develop. There are many circumstances in our lives, some good and some not so good that are meant to train us and raise us up.

Think of some things that you went through that God used to train and strengthen you.

_____

_____

Ask for God's help in prayer to use the difficult times to make you a stronger person.

_____

_____

_____

_____

THURSDAY
DAY 40

There are two things we can learn from David about our own lives when the bottom drops out.
1. He accepted what God was doing.
2. He did the best he could with what he had to work with.

Sometimes we get so despondent because things seem to be working against us. We begin to think we have lost all and have nothing left. This is paralyzing and also untrue.
Read Matthew 19:16-26

What kind of follower of Christ do you think that young man wanted to be?

_____

_____

Salvation is the most important need of man. Yet, it is something he cannot accomplish on his own. It is a work of God.
If God can accomplish salvation for a lost human being, don't you think He can do lesser miracles, like turn an empty life into a full life?

Do you remember the miracle of the feeding of the five thousand? He fed the multitude with two fish and five little loaves of bread. He can turn a little into a lot.

Here, God said to David, "Here is a cave."
David said, "I'll use it."
God said, "Here are some malcontents."
David said; "I'll take them."

What little do you have left that God can use to turn things around for you?

_____

_____

The progression of David went from:
1. His lowest point in life
2. On his knees
3. On his feet

Ask for God's help in prayer to accept whatever He is doing in your life and to use whatever you have left.

_____

_____

_____

_____

FRIDAY
DAY 41

We know that David was at his lowest point in a cave when he was running from Saul. We now find him on his knees.
Read Psalm 57

David is certainly not in a comfortable place. If he is talking about the malcontents who gathered themselves to him, they are not the best company. Miserable people are not fun people to be around. Malcontents are so overwhelmed with their own needs, they don't pay attention to anyone else's needs.

But David doesn't stay there, we find him on his feet.
I will bless the Lord at all times, His praise shall continually be in my mouth.
Psalm 34:1

In that dank, dark cave, David's men became the disciplined soldiers that would serve him and help rule Israel.

The Psalms are not only beautiful songs, of which we do not have the music today, but their message is impacting and everlasting.

When distressed, sing:
O taste and see that the Lord is good, how blessed is the man who takes refuge in Him. Psalm 34:8
When lacking, sing:
O fear the Lord, you His saints; for to those who fear Him, there is no want.
Psalm 34:9
When discontented, sing:
They who seek the Lord shall not be in want of any good thing. Psalm 34:10

Many of David's psalms were written during the lowest points of his life. He found comfort and hope from the inspiration he received from the Holy Spirit when writing them.

Ask for God's help in prayer to remind you to read a psalm in times of need.

_____

_____

_____

_____

SATURDAY
DAY 42

David had some low points in his life but there were many good things that were going to follow. It is the same with you. The lowest point in your life is not the end, it is the place of redirection. David shows us how to turn that curse into a beautiful blessing.

Many are the afflictions of the righteous, but the Lord delivers him out of them all. Psalm 34:19

Read John 16:32-33

Life for the disciples wasn't easy. Jesus foretold that they would encounter difficult times.

What does He say will happen to them?

_____

_____

Why does He tell them to take courage?

_____

_____

Jesus has gotten the victory over the world. When you are in Jesus you share that victory. When you walk with Jesus you experience that victory.

What is a victory you have gotten by walking with Jesus? It could be something you did that was right or something you didn't do that was wrong.

_____

_____

The conversion of a soul is the miracle of a moment but the making of a saint is the task of a lifetime.
God isn't about to give up, even when you are in such a cave. He is not through, even though you are at the lowest you have ever been.

Ask for God's help in prayer to lift you up when low.

_____

_____

_____

_____

WEEK EIGHT

Life can dish out a lot of pain. You don't have to be in this world very long before you can experience rejection, heartache, loss, or loneliness. And as much as any of these can hurt the heart of an individual, there is another experience that can hurt as much. Perhaps the reason this one hurts so much is because it didn't have to happen. We could call it "When you've been done wrong."

This week we will learn how to handle life after you have been wronged.

MONDAY
DAY 43

Saul is still on the hunt for David. He was jealous of David's popularity and it was driving him to end David's life. David was certainly undeserving of this treatment.
Read I Samuel 23:14-15

The human mind wrestles with the idea of God allowing the mistreatment of innocent people. It doesn't make sense to the natural mind.
Remember that God is preparing David to be the next king over Israel.
Read vs. 24-29

Sometimes God waits till the last minute to bring deliverance.
What did God do to deliver David?

_____

_____

How has God ever delivered you from something at the last minute?

_____

_____

In v.29, Engedi was a good place to hide. It consisted of rocks and caves and provided water, lush vegetation and a natural lookout against oncoming enemies.

David is, for now, safe and secure.

Ask for God's help in prayer to provide a safe place for you when being pursued by an enemy.

TUESDAY
DAY 44

There is a temptation in life that we believe, if we give in to it, will bring great satisfaction. Actually, all temptations deceive us into thinking that. But this one is different. It just comes so naturally. We see it all the time. It is the temptation to take revenge.

Read I Samuel 24:1-3

Passages like this stop anyone from accusing the Bible of being just a book written by man.

Saul picks a cave but not just any cave. David was in the same cave as Saul.

What do you think Davis's temptation was?

_____

_____

Read v.4

The sound of many voices can be very powerful.

What were David's men trying to get him to do?

_____

_____

David's men would soon be mighty men, but right now they are just carnal, fleshly men.

What situation, if any, have you ever been in where many voices were trying to get you to do something, but you felt it was wrong?

_____

_____

The carnal mind will always be ready to strike back when given the opportunity. Justified vengeance means I have been done wrong and it is okay to get even.

Ask for God's help in prayer about someone you feel like getting even.

_____

_____

_____

_____

WEDNESDAY
DAY 45

It is easy to say that God is "in something" when He really isn't. People often say God did this or God didn't come through. God gave me him or God gave me her. God gave me this job.
And then, when things don't work out we say, "God, how could You do this to me?"
All we are really doing is supporting our own idea by adding God to the mix.
Read I Samuel 24:4

Who did the men say set up this situation?

_____

It is dangerous to say that God is in everything. Even today He gets blamed for starving people, war, divorce, unemployment, etc.
Blaming God for our negative choices is like borrowing a car from someone and then blaming them because you cracked it up.

David wasn't perfect but he does offer us some wisdom for our own lives, especially the principle of how to handle the wrongs that have been done to us. He doesn't give in to the dictates of his men.

A famous missionary said,.
"Had I cared for the comments of people, I should have never been a missionary."   C.T. Studd

David did not take Saul's life but he did cut off a piece of the hem of his robe.
Read v.4

He did not give into the carnal influence but he still took matters into his own hands and his conscience bothered him.

The closer you walk with God the more sensitive the conscience.

It is easy to justify bad behavior.
Stealing a little box of paper clips from work can have the weight of an anchor when you walk closely with Jesus.

As you grow closer to Christ, your character means more than your desires.

Ask for God's help in prayer to stand against carnal comments.

THURSDAY
DAY 46

It is one thing not to be persuaded by carnal people to do the wrong thing. It is an even greater thing to persuade the carnal people not to do the wrong thing themselves.

Read I Samuel 24:6-7

David stood alone against four hundred men but his strong convictions were more powerful than the four hundred men together.

What did David use to persuade the men?

_____

David knew three things:
1. Saul was in the wrong but it was God's job to fix him.
2. He would have to stand alone in his convictions.
3. His confidence rested in God.

I'm sure he remembered the Old Testament teaching:

Vengeance is Mine and retribution, in due time their foot will slip. For the day of their calamity is near and the impending things are hastening upon them.

Deuteronomy 32:35

Ask for God's help in prayer to rest in Him for justice.

_____

_____

_____

_____

FRIDAY
DAY 47

It's important to make things right, even for the smallest infractions. We do this because we want to be clean and right before God and in our conscience. This is where we find David.

Read I Samuel 24:8-12

What evidence did David have that he could have taken Saul's life?

_____

_____

A test of real strength is not using it when you could. Restraint is the greater strength.

The wisdom of Solomon says,
> _He who is slow to anger is better than the mighty,_
> _And he who rules his spirit, than he who captures a city._ Proverbs 16:32

Is there something in your life now where you need restraint?

_____

_____

Read vs. 16-20

What did Saul say to David after this event?

_____

_____

Even Saul recognized the greatness of David. David's humility and ability to wait on God was stronger than wielding a sword.

Ask for God's help in prayer to make things right, even after the smallest incident.

_____

_____

_____

_____

SATURDAY
DAY 48

It is obvious that we are living in a fallen world. This causes great strife between people.
Read II Timothy 3:1-7

What are you to do with the kind of people mentioned there?

_____

Lessons learned this week:
Since man is depraved, expect to be mistreated.
Since mistreatment is inevitable, anticipate feelings of revenge.
Since the desire for revenge is predictable, refuse to fight in the flesh.

Retaliation is not freeing it is bondage and it never brings you to the level above "mere man." (just like everybody else)

We are not here to be like everybody else. We are here to be made Christlike.
The Apostle Paul said that we have a worthy life before us.
   Walk in a manner worthy of the calling with which you have been called.
                                                            Ephesians 4:1
And do this especially after you have been done wrong.

Ask for God's help in prayer especially after you have been done wrong.

_____

_____

_____

_____

WEEK NINE

Have you ever had the expectations from perhaps a job well done or a reward truly earned only to be completely let down? Could the way you felt be described as anger?

Anger is a debilitating state, it freezes the thinking and the emotions. This week we will see what happened to David when he received as a reward insults for a job well done.

MONDAY
DAY 49

It was customary in those days for wealthy men to hire shepherds to keep their flocks of sheep and goats. This was the time of year when the sheep were to be sheared and not only were the shepherds paid for their work but there would often be men who would protect the shepherds from wild tribes that would attack and steal.

It was an unwritten law or custom that these men would also be compensated for their protection.

Read I Samuel 25:1-6

David and his men had been faithfully watching the livestock of Nabal and protecting his shepherds. Sheep shearing is usually a time of lavish hospitality. People celebrated and guests were invited to the celebrations.

How is Abigail described?

_____

How is Nabal described?

_____

Do you consider yourself to have the character of Abigail or Nabal?

_____

In v. 6, what was David's attitude toward Nabal?

_____

You know something is coming tomorrow, but for today think about this scene. It is about a man doing a good deed for another man. He has high expectations of being thanked for his services. Anyone would probably have the same expectations.

Ask for God's help in prayer when it comes to the things that you expect in life.

_____

_____

_____

_____

TUESDAY
DAY 50

You work hard all week and expect to get paid for your services. Who wouldn't? This is where David was. He protected Nabal's livestock and workers. As was customary in that day, he expected to be rewarded.
Read I Samuel 25:5-9

In v.7, what is David saying he and his men did for Nabal?

_____

_____

In v.8, is David asking for a specific reward?

_____

_____

Read vs. 10-11

What is Nabal's reaction to David?

_____

_____

You can tell what kind of man Nabal is by his possessiveness. "My bread and my water and my meat that I have slaughtered for my shearers."

How would you describe Nabal's reaction to David?

_____

_____

How would you react if this happened to you?

_____

_____

Ask for God's help in prayer in handling your reactions to negative circumstances.

_____

_____

_____

_____

WEDNESDAY
DAY 51

Nabal's mistake was in thinking all that he had was because of him and for him. He did not understand that God's blessing to him should result in his blessing to others. This is a trap we never want to fall into.

Read Luke 12:16-21

In v.17, what similarity do you between the rich man and Nabal?

_____

_____

The rich man is talking to himself but he is not getting wisdom from God. So God begins to speak to him.

What does God say to him in v.20?

_____

_____

What is the lesson in v.21?

_____

_____

Ask for God's help in prayer to handle properly what you have been blessed with.

_____

_____

_____

_____

THURSDAY
DAY 52

David had a lot of patience up until now. He had lost his crutches. Saul was hunting for him. Four hundred malcontents attached themselves to him. But Nabal was really pushing his buttons.
Read I Samuel 25:11-13

What do you think David is about to do?

_____

_____

David took four hundred men with him. Seems like a little overkill.
Warning:
"When you deal with a fool, don't become a fool."
Write down that warning.

_____

_____

Anger is real, but don't let it destroy your self-control.

In the movie, "Forrest Gump," there is a particular scene with Jenny returning to her old home after her father has died and the old farm house is dilapidated and abandoned.
As she reflects on the sexual abuse she endured as a child, she is overcome by rage and begins throwing rocks at the house. She rapidly reaches for rocks and then violently throws them at the house.
Jenny finally falls to the ground in exhaustion and the scene closes with Forrest Gump philosophically saying, "Sometimes there just aren't enough rocks."
Ie.
Rage is difficult to satisfy, if not impossible. This is why we cannot give it a chanced to occur.

Read vs. 14-19

Impending doom was coming upon Nabal. He deserved what he was going to get. But Abigail did not let that happen because she was different. She did what was right. And she saved her husband's life and he didn't even know it.

Ask for God's help in prayer to give grace where people do not deserve it.

_____

_____

_____

_____

FRIDAY
DAY 53

Abigail was very different from her husband, Nabal.
Read I Samuel 25:20-25

Abigail possessed three wonderful qualities.
   1.   Tact – she humbled herself before David
What did she do in v.23 24?

_____

_____

   2.   Faith – She had faith that God was with David
What does she say in v.28?

_____

_____

   3.   Loyalty – to her husband.
She protected him and set out to prevent David from killing him.

Read vs. 32-34

What was David's response to what Abigail had done?

_____

_____

Remember we said in another chapter that vengeance belongs to the Lord? If we wait on God, He will bring justice.

Read vs. 36-38

What happened to Nabal?

_____

_____

Ask for God's help in prayer to give you patience to wait on Him.

_____

_____

_____

_____

SATURDAY
DAY 54

This was quite an event. Granted, the situation with sheep and shepherds may be far removed from your life today but the principle never grows old. Perhaps you had a fellow-feeling with David for a job you performed at work but your expectations of thanks were never fulfilled. If and when this does happen, there are three lessons for us.

1. Be wise.
Whenever you see conflict beginning to rise, be wise. If you handle conflict in the energy of the flesh, you will be sorry.
How to be wise:
- Weigh the facts
- Don't jump to conclusions
- Don't look at only your side
- Pray for wisdom

If any of you lacks wisdom, he should ask God. James 1:5

2. Be balanced.
- Take each conflict as it comes.
- Handle them as they arise
- Use fresh patience every day.

3. Be honest.
- When there is nothing you can do – wait.
- Restrain from doing anything hasty.

I waited patiently for the Lord and he inclined to me and heard my cry.
He brought me up out of the pit of destruction, out of the miry clay, and he set my
feet upon a rock making my footsteps firm. Psalm, 40:1-2

Your situation may not change but when you wait on God, you will change. You may even discover that while waiting, you learned that it was "you" who needed to change. This is the best way to handle anger.

Ask for God's help in prayer to check you every time you feel anger welling up inside.

———————————————————————————

———————————————————————————

———————————————————————————

———————————————————————————

WEEK TEN

Carnality is the enemy of every Christian. It is not something we ascribe to it is something we fall into. Like falling into a deep well, carnality is difficult to get out of, but it is possible.
This week we will see David's fall into carnality and his triumphal escape from it.

MONDAY
DAY 55

How does one go from being on top to the bottom? From being a winner to a loser? We do this by changing our thinking. You no longer think the thoughts that got you on top or made you the winner.

When you were a winner, you thought a certain way. When you changed the way you were thinking, you put yourself on the road to loser-ville. This is where we find David.

Up until now, David had been living in the promises of God. He had been thinking the thoughts of God.

Read I Samuel 27:1

What did David say that showed he was growing despondent?

_____

_____

Saul had left the cave where David had the opportunity to kill him and get rid of his problem once and for all. But he did not.

That was a great victory for David, not a military victory but for his integrity.

Sometimes our greatest defeats are on the threshold of our greatest victories. Those are usually the areas where we relax and put our guard down. The result is usually failure which leads to carnality.

Watch over your heart with all diligence,
For from it flow the springs of life. Proverbs 4:23

Ask for God's help in prayer to guard your heart.

_____

_____

TUESDAY
DAY 56

Sometimes our negative emotions are so strong, we forget who we really are in life. We forget what God has called us to and we even deny He has called us. David put his guard down regarding the calling on his own life.

Read I Samuel 27:2-4

David made two great mistakes.
1. He went back to the enemy of Israel.
2. He took others with him.

Who was the giant who formerly lived in Gath?

_____

What happened according to v. 4?

_____

_____

How easy it is to choose what we would consider the easy way out of a dilemma.

Have you ever considered the easy way out of a problem over the right way out?

_____

We could call this handling it the world's way rather than God's way. Warning;
Going back to the world only creates a false sense of security. Sin has its pleasures but only for a season.

Read v.5

What does David want to do?

_____

_____

Once in carnality, the only issue now is to make yourself comfortable. That is all that matters. It's the most important thing.
Read vs. 6-7

What city was David given to live in?

_____

How long did David and his men stay there?

_____

What might have been intended to be a short stay turned into a lengthy stay. Sometimes this leads to what we call "addiction."

Ask for God's help in prayer to avoid the easy way out.

_____

_____

_____

_____

WEDNESDAY
DAY 57

A long period of compromise leads to a lifestyle. Have you ever noticed that it is hard to get back into a routine after you have gotten out of it. Exercise, eating right, church attendance are all healthy routines but if you get out of those routines it is tough to get back in.

God had sent two angels to Lot who was living in Sodom and Gomorrah to warn him of God's coming judgment on their wickedness. They also said to Lot, "Run from the city and do not look back."
Read Genesis 19:15-26

What happened in v.26?

_____

The sons-in-law didn't believe Lot that God was going to destroy the city and his daughters hesitated. Do you think Lot's testimony for God was serious enough to warrant belief in what he said? Maybe not.

Why do you think Lot's wife looked back?

_____

_____

When you live in the system of the world, it is hard to get back with God. Lot's family had gotten very comfortable there.
David also had gotten comfortable in Gath. He had gotten out of the habit of praying, singing and writing psalms.

He couldn't sing the Lord's songs while living in the devil's land.

What routine have you ever gotten out of and found it difficult to get back into?

_____

_____

Ask for God's help in prayer to get back into any broken, healthy routine.

_____

_____

_____

_____

THURSDAY
DAY 58

Carnality creates an identity crisis. On the outside a person is worldly and on the inside he or she is Christian. David had this crisis.

Carnality leads to loss. David's first loss is his identity.
On the outside he was carnal and on the inside he was an Israelite. There is no peace when God's people live this way.

The second loss is his acceptance.
Read I Samuel 29:1-5

What is coming under question here?

_____

_____

David no longer fits in with his new associates.
Read vs. 6-7

What does Achish tell David to do?

_____

When someone goes back to the world it is only a matter of time before they are rejected there too.
Read Luke 15:11-16

Ask for God's help in prayer through your identity loss.

_____

_____

_____

_____

FRIDAY
DAY 59

We've been talking about the losses people experience when living in carnality. They lose their true identity because they are like two people. They lose their acceptance because they don't really fit in anywhere. Today we will examine two more losses David experienced and hopefully learn some lessons for our own lives.

Previously we saw that David and his men and their families were living in Ziklag.
Read I Samuel 30:1-4

What was taken from David?

_____

_____

David's third loss was his family and the families of his men.
Whenever someone sins, it is never to themselves. Other people always experienced the consequences and usually the ones closest.

The fourth thing David lost was the trust of his men.
Read v.6

What did David's men want to do to him?

_____

Can you see how what looks like taking the easy way out is not the easy way out?

What have you ever lost from times of being carnal?

_____

_____

Reminder,

When we speak of being carnal it has to do with our thinking. We think human thoughts rather than divine thoughts: man's ways rather than God's ways.

Then the carnal thoughts lead to carnal actions. Regret usually follows.

Ask for God's help in prayer with your thought life.

_____

_____

_____

_____

SATURDAY
DAY 60

We can all agree now that carnality is a bad place to be. It is very costly and creates all kinds of problems for the individual and those in their inner circle. The good news is that no one has to stay there. There is a way out.

Read I Samuel 30:6

At the end of the verse, what did David do?

_____

_____

David didn't stay in his pit. He may have left God but God never left him. We never want to forget God's divine mercy.

Is it any wonder David could write Psalm 86?
  You are forgiving and good, O Lord, abounding in love to all who call on you.
                                                                        v.5
But Thou, O Lord, art a God merciful and gracious, slow to anger and abundant in lovingkindness and truth.   v.15

Can you think of a time when God was forgiving and merciful to you?

_____

_____

Thank God for His mercy and forgiveness in a prayer.

_____

_____

WEEK ELEVEN

God has a perfect will and He has a permissive will. This perfect will is what He desires while His permissive will is what he allows. Man has a free will and the choices we make can vacillate between those two types of will. When we live in God's permissive will we usually have an ending that didn't have to be. This week we will be schooled in choosing God's perfect will and doing our best to avoid and end that didn't have to be.

MONDAY
DAY 61

When someone lives in carnality, you could say they are "playing the fool."

Seventeenth Century author, J. Sidlow Baxter makes these remarks regarding playing the fool.

A man plays the fool when:

- He goes on enterprises for God before God sent him.
- He disobeys God even in seemingly small matters.
- He tries to cover up disobedience to God with religious excuses.
- He tries to persuade himself that he is doing the will of God when in his heart he knows he is not.
- He allows some jealousy or hatred to master him.
- He knowingly fights against God to save his own face.
- He turns from God and seeks an alternative.

Have you ever fallen into any of these actions?

_____

_____

Read I Samuel 26:21

The Bible is very clear about the actions of a fool.
Doing wickedness is like sport to a fool,
And so is wisdom to a man of understanding. Proverbs 10:23

Leave the presence of a fool,
or you will not discern words of knowledge. Proverbs 14:7

A rebuke goes deeper into one who has understanding
Than a hundred blows to a fool. Proverbs 17:10

A fool does not delight in understanding,
But only in revealing his own mind. Proverbs 18:2

Better is a poor man who walks in his integrity,
than he who is perverse in speech and is a fool. Proverbs 19:1

Perhaps the most sobering of all:
The fool has said in his heart,
"There is no God." Psalm 14:1

Ask for God's help in prayer that you never play the fool.

_____

_____

_____

_____

TUESDAY
DAY 62

As we follow the life of King Saul we see that carnality is progressive and there is a final stage to it – death.
Read I Samuel 31:1-6

Saul was wounded in battle and his sons, including Jonathan, were killed.
Read v. 7

What did the Israelites do?

_____

What did the Philistines do?

_____

Read vs. 8-9

What did the Philistines do to Saul?

_____

_____

This was a tragic scene. Yet, an even greater tragedy is that it didn't have to be. Saul never had to die like this.

Carnality is living outside the blessing of God.

Ask for God's help in prayer that you never backslide like Saul.

_____

_____

_____

WEDNESDAY
DAY 63

Saul made a series of poor choices with his life. He became jealous and acted on it. He let murder reign in his heart and left his rightful place as ruler over Israel to pursue his own desires, to kill David. His ending was an ending that didn't have to be.

Read Matthew 6:22-23

Jesus is talking about perception. If we look at life with a distorted view, we will make distorted decisions. If we look at life in the light of God, we will see clearly and make better decisions.

If your eye is bad, what is your body full of?

_____

If your eye is clear, what is your body full of?

_____

What is the danger of confusing darkness with light?

_____

_____

The carnal path always leads to destruction. It begins as a thought and progresses to an action.

Ask for God's help in prayer to keep your eye clear.

_____

_____

_____

_____

THURSDAY
DAY 64

Life is filled with surprises, some good and some not so good. There will also be some surprises when we enter into eternity, some good and some not so good.
Read Matthew 7:21-23

In v.21, what does it take to enter into heaven?

_____

What is the surprise in v.23?

_____

Why did Jesus tell them to depart?

_____

In the words of F.B. Meyer;
"This is the bitterest of all – to know that suffering need not have been: that it has resulted from indiscretion and inconsistency; that it is the harvest of one's own sowing; that the vulture which feeds on the vitals is a nestling of one's own rearing. Ah me! This is pain!"

Are you sure of your entrance into heaven?

_____

How do you know?

_____

_____

Pray a prayer asking Jesus to be your Savior.

_____

_____

FRIDAY
DAY 65

Believe it or not there is an analogy between Christ's death and Saul's death. God's word is given to us so we can have hope.
Read Romans 15:4

Why were the Scriptures written for us?

_____

_____

The analogy:
Saul's death appeared to be the end of all national hope.
When Saul died, people thought that was the end of Israel.
When Christ died people thought that was the end of the hope of the coming kingdom.

It seemed as if the adversary had won,
The Philistines displayed Saul's head in triumph.
The Romans displayed Christ's body on a cross.

 Saul's death paved the way for an entirely new plan of operation. It opened the way for the kingly line of David.
Christ's death opened up the way of salvation.

Saul's death opened up an opportunity for another king to rule.
When Christ died, He opened up a way for the church to evangelize the world.

Saul's death ended an era of dissatisfaction and failure.
Christ's death ended an era of law and guilt introducing a new arrangement of Grace.

Saul's death displayed the foolishness of man.

Christ's death displayed the foolishness of God.
(human understanding)

> *For the word of the cross is to those who are perishing foolishness,*
> *but to us who are being saved it is the power of God.* I Corinthians 1:18

Pray a prayer of thanksgiving for all that God has done.

_____

_____

_____

_____

SATURDAY
DAY 66

We read the Word of God to receive instructions for this life. We want a healthy, wholesome life and a grand entrance into eternity. The dangers of carnality are real and can offset the whole journey.
Read I Timothy 1:18-19

What kind of fight are we to fight?

_____

What kind of conscience are we to have?

_____

What will happen if we do not?

_____

Final warning:
Do not compromise your convictions.
Keep your Christian testimony strong.
Do not live a carnal life.
Choose the right way not the easy way.
Be a light in this dark world.

Ask for God's help in prayer to keep you on track.

_____

_____

_____

_____

WEEK TWELVE

We come to the conclusion of our study of the life of David, a man with a heart after God. This week we will see what it means to have a heart after God and how to get one.

MONDAY
DAY 67

David is one of the more popular characters of the Bible. When you hear the name David, you usually associate it with Goliath, Bathsheba and Jonathan.
In spite of David's failures, the Apostle Paul leaves us in the New Testament with a commentary that sums up the life of David the way God sees it.
Read Acts 13:16-22

God didn't mention David's fighting skills, brilliant leadership or even his many wives. Rather, He leaves us with the thought that David cares about the things that God cares about.
What did God say He found?

_____

_____

God is interested in His will. That is because it is His divine purpose for man on the earth.
What do you think God thinks about the man or woman who wants to do His will?

_____

_____

To be after God's heart then is to be after what God is after. It is having the same value system as God.
Rate yourself from 1 to 10 on living for God's will.
       1 2   3 4 5 6 7 8 9 10
Why do you think you chose the number you did?

_____

_____

Having a heart after God is serving God with joy. It is not doing God's will grudgingly, but joyfully.

You do it joyfully because it is important to you because it is important to God.

Ask for God's help in prayer give you a heart like His.

_____

_____

_____

_____

TUESDAY
DAY 68

The Ark of the Covenant was a wooden chest overlaid with gold. It contained the tablets of the Ten Commandments, a pot of manna and Aaron's rod. Two golden statues of angels faced each other overlooking the mercy seat on the top of the Ark. Actually, they were looking down at the mercy seat on the Ark.

The Ark came to signify the presence and blessing of God. It was so important to the Lord that he gave Moses specific instructions on how to build it.

The Ark was actually the holiest place on earth because it represented the presence of Jehovah.

When David took the throne the people had become lukewarm in their faith. Their hearts were anything but after God.

Read II Samuel 1-6

The moving of the Ark was a sacred responsibility. Human hands were not allowed to touch the Ark. Poles were constructed to lift and carry it.

At each corner was a ring of gold through which a pole was slide on either side. The poles would be placed on the shoulders of the Levites (priests) to transport the Ark.

What were the people doing in v.5?

_____

_____

God's presence is worthy of celebration.

We don't have the Ark in our presence today but we do have the presence of Jesus. He is worthy of our rejoicing. When you come to church on Sunday, come with a spirit of rejoicing. It is truly a time of praise and celebration for what He has done for us.

Of course there are times when you come to church and your heart is heavy. But Sunday is about Him, and He deserves all of our attention.

God knows what you have need of. But you also need to worship Him because that is what brings refreshing to your soul.

Ask for God's to give you a spirit of rejoicing and worship when you go to church on Sunday.

_____

_____

_____

_____

WEDNESDAY
DAY 69

The end doesn't justify the means. I'm sure you have heard that before. It means that the result is not greater than how you get there. God is more interested in how you get things done than in what you actually get done.
You can make a lot of money but doing it dishonestly doesn't impress God. You can share your faith but doing it in a condemning way doesn't impress God.
So you see, it how we do things that is very important.
Read II Samuel 6:6-7

David seemed to be hastily moving the Ark and the oxen stumbled and the Ark began to shake.
What did Uzzah do?

_____

What did God do to Uzzah?

_____

How did David respond?

_____

David probably thought he had a right to be angry at God but Uzzah broke the rules. The Ark was sanctified and only the priests could move it and that, with poles. No one was allowed to touch the Ark.

Doing a right thing in a wrong way doesn't make it right.

If you are serving God that is a beautiful thing but even that must be done His way.

Getting into heaven is very important but we can only get in one way, God's way. Too many people are trying to get there their own way but they will never make it.

Jesus Himself said;

I am the way the truth and the life.
No one comes to the Father but by me. John 14:6

God the Father knows what He is doing.

Ask for help in prayer when you serve Him that you would do so His way.

_____

_____

_____

_____

THURSDAY
DAY 70

We hear a lot of talk about Glorifying God, and we should. But what does that mean? Some think it is doing things for God and then saying "I give God the glory." Actually, it is more than that. Glorifying God is doing what you do His way. It is serving with a loving heart and a right attitude. We meet up with David and he has a bad attitude.

Read II Samuel 6:6-10

Why did David become angry?

_____

Being a man after God's heart doesn't mean you are perfect. It means you are sensitive, and when you are wrong you own up to it.

David didn't do his homework.
What was his question in v.9?

_____

What do you think the answer is?

_____

(I would say, have the priests move it)

We have to be careful we do not run out and do God's work without first discovering how He wants it done.

Someone says;
I want to follow after God.
   No one who puts his hand to the plow and looks back is fit for the kingdom of
                       God. Luke 10:62
I want to really love God.

If anyone comes to Me and does not hate his father and mother, his wife and children, his brothers and sisters – yes, even his own life, he cannot be My disciple.
Luke 14:26

I want to walk with Jesus.

If anyone would come after Me, he must deny himself and take up his cross and follow me. Mark 8:34

What really matters is what God's Word says. He determines the way in which things are to be done.

Ask for help in prayer when to see the seriousness of following Jesus.

_____

_____

_____

_____

FRIDAY
DAY 71

When we begin to care about the things God cares about, we begin to desire to do those things His way. This is taking God seriously. This is becoming men and women after God's heart.

David didn't move the Ark for three months. Finally, he remembered only the Levites (priests) could move the Ark using poles slipped through the golden rings on the corners. The Ark was then moved successfully with great rejoicing.
Read II Samuel 6:12-15

This was a great celebration but somebody didn't like what David was doing.
Read vs.14-16

Read vs. 20-23

Michal, David's wife made two mistakes.
1. She chose her father, Saul over her husband, David.
2. She despised him for dancing before the Lord.

What happened to Michal in v.23?

_____

_____

This could be for one of two reasons:
1. She was under divine discipline from God.
2. David was no longer intimate with her.

Perhaps this teaches us we don't always have to be reserved in our worship. The more you have to be thankful for, the more joy you will express.

When you go to worship on Sunday don't be afraid to clap your hands, lift your hands, raise your voice. It is an expression of joy for who God is and what He has done.

Ask for help in prayer when you express yourself in worship.

_____

_____

_____

_____

SATURDAY
DAY 72

Our journey is a never-ending journey of learning. What have we learned from David and Michal?

David's eyes were on the Lord.
Michal's eyes were on other people. What would they think!

We can make an application:
1. The better you know where you stand with the Lord, the freer you can be.

It was for freedom that Christ set us free; therefore keep standing firm and do not be subject again to a yoke of slavery. Galatians 5:1

What freedoms have you been enjoying since you became a Christian?

_____

_____

To be free, learn the Scriptures and then live in them.

2. Freedom in God breeds confidence in self.
David was confident in himself but because Michal wasn't confident in herself, she despised what David did instead of enjoying his freedom with him.

3. Be conscious of the little things.
The little gold rings on the corners of the Ark may seem insignificant but they played a huge role in moving the Ark. Don't over-look the little things in your life.

The little things that you do right and are faithful in will be rewarded. This is what will make you Godly husbands and wives, Godly workmen, Godly musicians, Godly professionals, Godly managers, etc.

Whoever can be trust with very little can also be trusted with much.
Jesus   Luke 16:10

Ask for help in prayer to empower you to live in what you learned in this devotional.

_____

_____

_____

_____

CONGRATULATIONS

You have completed a seventy-two day spiritual journey through the devotional,
"David, A Man With A Heart After God."
My prayer is that it has been a blessing and a challenge to you to go the extra mile in your faith. It is truly an worthwhile effort.
May God bless you as you continue your journey.
In Christ's love,
Pastor Dave Therrien

About The Author

David P. Therrien

Graduated from Gordon Conwell Seminary in Boston, MA with a Masters of Arts Degree In Urban Ministry. He enjoys the four seasons of New England with his wife, Donna and has three sons, Michael, David Jr. and Alex.

Dave writes on matters of faith and encouragement and pastors the wonderful people of New Hope Christian Church in Swansea, MA.

www.newhopecc.tv

MEDIA
Check out Dave's radio show
WARV 1590 am dial
Or
Stream it at
WARV.net
Weekdays at 12:30 pm E.T. and
Saturdays at 3 pm.

DVDs & CDs can also be found at
www.newhopecc.tv
MEDIA button

POCKETBOOK SERIES
So far...

Look Up And Be Forgiven VOL. 1

Going Forward In Faith VOL. 2

How To Escape From Guilt & Shame VOL. 3

Grace, Kindness & Righteousness VOL. 4

The Loving Father & The Lost Son VOL. 5

The Brightest Future Ever VOL. 6

My Spiritual Journey VOL. 7

A Christmas Reflection VOL. 8

Broken Things VOL. 9

Proverbs For Men VOL. 10

Proverbs For Women VOL. 11

Broken Things VOL. 12

OTHER BOOKS
So far...

Beauty In Darkness
Finding HOPE In Distressing Times

GOT Life?
How To Know If You're Really Living

Angel Conversations
A Journey Through Popular Bible Stories

Sailing Through Storms

Recovering Lost Ground
*A 12 Step Guide to Overcoming
Compulsive Behaviors*

Leaving A Godly Legacy
How You Will Be Remembered After You Are Gone

Bible Men Study Guide
With DVD

Questions About Salvation

Homosexuality
Good Choice or Bad Choice?

Think Twice
About What You're Going To Say Or Do
40 Day Reading Guide

Life is a journey,
Don't look back and keep moving.